Minibeast Poems

Compiled by John Foster

Conten

Acknowledgements
The Editor and Publisher wish to thank the following who have kindly given permission for the use of copyright material:

Lynette Craig for 'Spider in the bath' © 1993 Lynette Craig; John Kitching for 'Fly' © 1993 John Kitching; Daphne Lister for 'The wuzzy wasps of Wasperton' from BBC Poetry Corner © 1989 Daphne Lister; Tony Mitton for 'Ladybird, ladybird' © 1993 Tony Mitton; Brian Moses for 'Ants' © 1993 Brian Moses; Judith Nicholls for 'A bluebottle is' and 'Water boatman' both © 1993 Judith Nicholls and for 'Stick insect' © 1990 Judith Nicholls, previously published in 'Higgledy-humbug' (Mary Glasgow Publications); J. Walsh for 'Minibeasts' © 1993 J. Walsh.

The wuzzy wasps of Wasperton

The wuzzy wasps of Wasperton
Are buzzing round the plums
And sucking all the juicy ones
Before somebody comes.

2

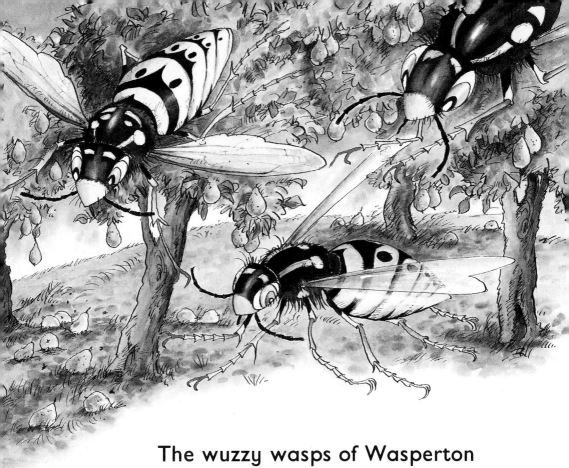

The wuzzy wasps of Wasperton
Are buzzing round the pears
And choosing all the ripest ones—
They think the orchard's theirs.

The wuzzy wasps of Wasperton
Steal fruit fit for a king.
But don't disturb them if you go—
Those wuzzy wasps can STING!

Daphne Lister

3

Fly

Fly, fly, please go away.
Please go away I beg.
You've nibbled at my nose.
You've nibbled at my leg.

4

You've tickled toes and ears and arms.
You've wandered on my food.
You've dipped into my lemonade.
You're really rather rude.

I must insist you go away,
You are an awful pain.
Buzz off! Annoy some quiet cow!
And don't come back again!

John Kitching

5

Ants

Dad says I've got ants in my pants
when I can't sit still at all,
but the only ants I ever see
are crawling on our garden wall.

Brian Moses

6

Spider in the bath

I've picked up frogs,
And patted dogs,
Stroked the skin of snakes.
I've tickled cats,
Examined bats,
Fed the ducks and drakes.

I've chased fat hens,
Pushed sheep in pens,
Held chickens in my hand.
Been stung by bees
On both my knees,
Pulled crabs out of the sand.

I've watched a mole
Go down his hole,
Followed ants along a path.
So why am I
So frightened of
A spider in the bath?

Lynette Craig

A bluebottle is

A bluebottle is
a buzz,
a whizz!
He's faster than you,
a dazzle of blue,
that's what he is!

A bluebottle is
a buzz,
a whizz,
a dive,
a zoom,
a catch-if-you-can,
a rocket for one,
THAT'S what he is!

Judith Nicholls

Stick insect

Pick an insect,
stick an insect
on the kitchen floor.
Which is insect,
which is twig?
Who knows any more!

Judith Nicholls

Water boatman

Across the pond
the boatman rows.
Where he came from
nobody knows.

He dips and dives
from space to space.
The pond is still,
he loves to race!

What can he see
as he darts by?
Below, dark weeds.
Above, blue sky.

Across the pond
the boatman rows.
Where is he going?
Nobody knows!

Judith Nicholls

13

Minibeasts

The ants rush around
from lawn to nest,
they never stop
to have a rest.

The spiders cast webs
from flower to bush,
they are never seen working
or in a rush.

The dragonflies hover
high and low,
they never seem sure
of which way to go.

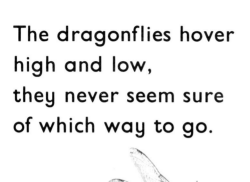

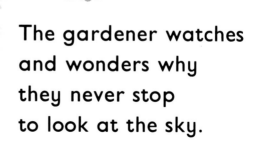

The gardener watches
and wonders why
they never stop
to look at the sky.

John Walsh

15

Ladybird, ladybird

Ladybird, ladybird,
don't fly away.
Live in my garden,
I want you to stay.

I've little green bugs
all over my trees.
So come back and eat them
ladybird, please.

Tony Mitton

16